D1461454

TIME TO CALL HOME

Time to Call Home

HUGH O'DONNELL

VERITAS

Published 2021 by
Veritas Publications
7–8 Lower Abbey Street
Dublin 1, Ireland

publications@veritas.ie
www.veritas.ie

ISBN 978-1-84730-962-4

A catalogue record for this book is available from the British
Library.

Illustrations by Beth O'Halloran
Designed by Lir Mac Cárthaigh, Veritas Publications
Cover designed by Jeannie Swan, Veritas Publications
Cover image: 'Tulips in Golden Light' by Karl Gaff
Printed in Ireland by Print Media Services, Dublin

Veritas books are printed on paper made from the wood pulp
of managed forests. For every tree felled, at least one tree is
planted, thereby renewing natural resources.

For Auntie Mary, my godmother,
who made music of her life.

ACKNOWLEDGEMENTS

A special word of thanks to Aidan Mathews, former producer of RTÉ Radio's 'A Living Word' in which a number of these reflections were first given voice, and to Pat Egan, editor of *The Salesian Bulletin,* for airing many of them as 'Songs for the Slow Lane'. To Karl Gaff for his glowing cover image and to Beth O'Halloran for her delicate lines I am deeply grateful. In a wider sense, I would like to express my gratitude to the many people who in various ways have inspired me to care deeply for God's creation, though inevitably with hardly the faintest appreciation of how seriously God cares for the wondrous being of every creature.

Nature is filled with words of love, but how can we listen to them amid constant noise, interminable and nerve-wracking distractions, or the cult of appearances?

Pope Francis, *Laudato Si'*, 225

If we fall in love with creation deeper and deeper, we will respond to its endangerment with passion.

Hildegard of Bingen

CONTENTS

Introduction 13

1. TAKING STOCK

Earthing 20

A Beckoning 22

Leaf Time 24

A Benedictine Welcome 26

Wabi Sabi.. 28

Bee Orchid 30

An Exaltation 32

St Fachtna's Well 34

Earthly Music 36

Blossom... 38

Tomato Festival....................................... 40

Mist 42

Joshua Bell 44

Among Trees... 46

Love Story.. 48

Come and Have Breakfast 50

En Plein Air.. 52

2. WHY ARE YOU PERSECUTING ME?

Mermaid 56

Birdsong on the Western Front 58

Air Pollution 60

Holy Ground 62

People Like Berta Cáceres 64

Curious Creatures 66

Fearfully and Wonderfully Made 68

Goats as Gardeners 70

Another Christmas Morning 72

Doris Salcedo at IMMA 74

Swifts 76

The Age of Plastic 78

100 Animals to See Before They Die 80

Road Kill 82

Cementing the Garden 84

Musical Parents 86

Unheard Melody 88

3. UNLESS YOU BECOME LIKE LITTLE CHILDREN

Earth Child..92

Frankie 94

'My Daddy is Weird'................................96

Watch Me..98

A Pail of Water......................................100

The Reason I Jump...............................102

Planet Dancing......................................104

Such Company......................................106

Three Little Pigs....................................108

Jasmine..110

A Ribbon for Brigid...............................112

Dead Fox..114

Words in their Jackets...........................116

Alice at Five...118

All Sleeping Things................................120

The Unseeable Animal 122

Naughty Face...124

4. CALLING HOME

An Aftertaste.............................. 128
As the Postman Said...................... 130
Soil Mates................................. 132
Going....................................... 134
Cactus..................................... 136
The Story Goes 138
'Have You Caught Anything?'.............. 140
Prayer Plant.............................. 142
Consuela................................... 144
Let There Be Light 146
Wild Garlic 148
Baking Bread 150
Red Shoes.................................. 152
Fruits and Nuts........................... 154
Adlestrop 156
A Messenger............................... 158
You Called................................ 160

INTRODUCTION

'*M*ind the gap' is a phrase we have come to associate with public transport. As the station approaches, the warning is issued, the gap in question being the sometimes generous step between platform and door.

But the phrase has another possible reference; this time to the growing gap between ourselves and the natural world. More and more, it seems, we are drifting apart, splitting up. Children seldom 'go out to play' in open spaces anymore and most of us, at every free moment, feel the need to check our phones or simply graze on social media.

Meanwhile, we go on polluting every corner of our world and destabilising our climate by the wasteful, thoughtless way we are living. And Earth is not home to us in any real affectionate sense except at those grand moments when, caught unawares, we are silenced by a sunset, by the shock of a night sky sequinned with stars, or when confronted by the presence of another creature.

When Rachel Carson wrote *Silent Spring* in 1962, she was describing what happens when we spray the wayside plants with pesticides; how the poison runs from leaf to soil to worm to bird – and birdsong dies! She was saying that we do not need to deliver a direct hit to do real damage to the living world.

The gap widens. Still Earth calls to us in every leaf, rock and insect to come home, to be homemakers, to remember that all of us belong here together as family and nowhere else.

Wonder, trust, gratitude: these are the qualities required to enter the kingdom of heaven on earth. We are meant to be bowled over, to be amazed, to find bliss. But for this to happen we must pay attention and return to our senses (and responsibilities) if we are to 'Grow with nature again as before I grew' (Patrick Kavanagh, 'Canal Bank Walk').

This sequence of interweaving meditations is arranged in four sections. The first reminds us of the beauty and diversity of life and how earlier humans appreciated the sacredness of their shared living space with a sensitivity we have all but lost. The second focuses on the suffering we inflict on ourselves and other creatures through war, injustice, disrespect and how the earth then becomes a dumping ground for a generation addicted to endless consumption. The third returns us to our need for play and storytelling, to being the embodied, responsive children that we essentially are. The last section has an elegiac tone with the subtext that, sadly, we do not know what we've got until it's gone, whether that be species, habitat, friendship or way of life.

We are Earth Beings who have gone astray. It's time to call home.

— 1 —
TAKING STOCK

When you bring your attention to a
stone, a tree or an animal,
you can sense how still it is, and in
doing so, the same stillness arises
within you.

Eckhart Tolle, *Silence Speaks:*
Whispers of Now

EARTHING

'*T*ell me that story; you know the one,'
I say to Angela, who has lived among
the Aboriginal people of Australia for
forty years, and she recounts how, after
an outdoor celebration of the Eucharist
on a dry riverbed, one of the women
Elders had confided to her, 'There was
not enough silence for me to hear the
footsteps from the Elders of the past
forty thousand years.'

Our rituals tend to be overburdened with
words as if silence were alien to us. And we
forget that from the beginning the Creator
has been speaking in different voices to our
ancestors as they came to know themselves
as wedded to the earth and keyed in to how
everything is related. 'The birds are true
friends,' her neighbour would say.

Angela goes on to explain that these are not superstitions but realities for people whose lives are marked with a deep sense of belonging. So, you never blunder in but seek permission from the spirits to walk a particular stretch of earth.

We think we can live without such connections but we are out of touch. Dust never clings to our feet. By comparison, we don't know who we are or where we come from or that all this matters. We kill the silence.

There are layers of belonging. The 'giant leap for mankind', according to the pilgrim-poet, John Moriarty, is not leaving a boot print on the moon but rather setting foot on the earth, as if for the first time, and calling it home.

A BECKONING

*G*oing in to the Big Fern House in the Botanic Gardens in Dublin you descend some steps. On one of them is a plaque which states that in the winter of 1948–9 the Swiss philosopher, Ludwig Wittgenstein, while living in Dublin, came often to sit there and write. Two years later he was dead.

Whenever I visit the glasshouse of the large tropical plants I think of him watched over by the surrounding vegetation adapting to life away from home. Coffee plants, banana trees, cycads and bamboo with their storylines and lifestyles as accomplished as our own.

Maybe that's why Mr Wittgenstein's memory is important to me. It's usual to think that he was pondering some knotty existential conundrum but maybe he was just happily being there among such exotic creatures and learning from them how to be more himself.

I even wonder was he growing to love their company and were they noticing that *he* was back again, *over there on the step*. To think that they wouldn't notice shows how little we know of what it means to be alive. In our own hurry through are we not often the ones least alive?

The other day I could hear birdsong in there and felt like Adam struggling for names in an alien world. Wittgenstein's well-known remark came to me then: 'About what we do not know we must be silent.' But silence is not simply an opposite. It is a beckoning, an atmosphere, a true account.

LEAF TIME

*T*he new leaves of the plant un-scroll.
I follow their progress over days; six
new leaves tightly packed lie deep in the
ballet of their unfolding. I am a witness
to a world beyond me.

A light green leaf invites, 'Read me.' But I
have to admit I am illiterate in leaf-time
and back away from this living text, this
inspired word. 'But it's only a leaf,' you
chide. 'What's so special about that?'

Leaf is the place of encounter, I try to
explain, between our sun and the family
of life. It is its ability to capture sunlight
and use it to make food that makes leaf
work so mind-blowing. And though gifted
in our generation to 'know' how that
chemistry works in the chloroplasts – a

mesmerising process – we cannot get beyond amazement.

Perhaps we may go to the tree and expect it will be easier to grasp this larger body. But if we can't appreciate the leaf, can we appreciate the tree? And without the alphabet of wonder, have we any hope of hearing the voice that reaches out to us in this un-scrolling, 'whose language is not our language', to reapply the words of R.S. Thomas as he listens to blackbird song.

To read a leaf means to be present before its mystery; to begin to understand how little we know; to imagine that we stand before a doorway that opens out in astonishment and opens inwards to deep joy; that there is something mystical about a leaf!

A BENEDICTINE WELCOME

*M*y first morning, I wake early and look out. For a moment, I think birds, swallows maybe, but quickly realise they are bats in a last fly-by before turning in for the day, their night shift over. In those few moments, I realise what a gift I have received as witness to these creatures having their last fling with the half-light before dreamtime.

I can't say there is something monk-like about them but, being at Glenstal, it's hard to resist some comparison. Perhaps a shared hidden life, an alternative programme, an intention to praise by being what they are – bats or monks.

'In the morning let me know your love', they pray, 'for I put my trust in you. Make me know the way I should walk.' Four times a day they meet in the chapel to chant, to do this work of reclaiming and holding this time as sacred. It is a human cry rising up from the awareness of who we are and how deep our need.

As a guest, I am smitten by the welcome I receive to join in their life's rhythm: 'Come eat with us, pray with us.' Later, while walking a woodland path past a stand of foxgloves or watching ducks being family on the lake, a sense of inner order is restored, some anxiety filtered as light flows in.

At twilight, of course, I will be waiting, hoping to see the brief shapes of pipistrelle slip silently from the roof space into the night.

WABI SABI

*A*fter breakfast I find myself looking at the side plate that I often use and seeing it, as it were, for the first time with its colourful image of fruits in a bowl.

Is it not surprising, then, that a painting, unrecognised as a Caravaggio, could hang for years in a Jesuit community in Dublin without attracting much attention. They knew the story of the arrest of Jesus well, had heard it from childhood so maybe didn't pay it much heed. Maybe a cleaner, as a humorous line suggests, even reached up a damp mop to wipe the dust off it from time to time.

However, when we declare something to be a masterpiece, priceless or holy, often we can overlook the point that the deep mystery of life is everywhere if we have eyes and ears for it and words of praise.

There is a man in a hi-vis jacket who cleans our street. I often hear him whistling to himself as he goes by. We greet each other while the morning rush hour hurries people along. What heavy thoughts are they carrying? What plans?

The Japanese have the word *wabi sabi* to describe a philosophy of sufficiency and restraint such as you find in their Tea Ceremony. It translates as a way of living where the humble, down-to-earth realities are valued above what is large and expensive. The grain in old wood or the sound of rain rinsing the trees triggers joy. Or the sight of a familiar plate.

BEE ORCHID

*W*alking across sand dunes on the west coast of Donegal, I think of Michael Longley's poem, 'The Ice-Cream Man', written to commemorate the ice-cream man who was murdered on the Lisburn Road. He had heard about the shooting on his return from a field trip to the Burren; his daughter had placed a bunch of carnations outside the shop. In addition to the list of ice-cream flavours that she knew by heart, he also included in his poem all the wild flowers he had seen in a day.

Around us are masses of lady's bedstraw, eyebright, yellow rattle, patches of common centaury, milkwort, sheep's sorrel and then, like a gift offered, the wonderful bee orchid. Two of them! And nearby three more!

'We were drawn to it,' someone said, and that was closer to what had happened than our own discovering of this rare creature for whom we get down on our hands and knees for a closer look.

A botanist friend, John Feehan, describes his first meeting with the bee orchid at the age of thirteen as 'heart-stopping', as a moment of revelation. Fifty years later, I can sense what he meant.

Our footprint grows heavier upon the earth. Maybe wild flowers can heal us if we let them. The Master understood as much when he said, 'attend to them' for in their beauty is revealed something of the Father's love. In their presence we are invited to be still.

AN EXALTATION

While awaiting execution, Roger Casement wrote to his sister recalling that moment of 'swimming ashore on an unknown strand' to a homecoming which caused him to be 'happy for the first time for over a year ... The sand hills were full of skylarks rising in the dawn, the first I had heard for years ... as I waded through the breakers ... I was back in Ireland.'

Returning to familiar sand dunes in summer recently with the air above us colonised and redefined by the sound of skylarks, we catch something of his emotion. If ever singing could be described as joyous, it must be this. And how they soar and fall, showing off to each other, we imagine, in a game of 'bet you can't do that'.

We stand amazed as a skylark rises from the ground and performs an aeronautic display just above us, the brilliance of his achievement to manage strong wind and almost walk on air leaving us dumbstruck. But it is not primarily for us.

It is obviously for his own joy and purpose and that of his companion on the ground that this disclosure takes place. And it cannot be described, although our words, like the earthen vessels that they are, attempt, and fail, to hold this treasure.

Mesmerised, we listen and watch as he sketches out a meaning in wing beat, check and glide. Gestures to which the word 'worship' might apply, the bird being what it embodies – divine goodness outsourced as skylark, its warm breast rising and falling, rising and falling.

ST FACHTNA'S WELL

A disc of sky almost blinks back
at me like one blue eye. This is
St Fachtna's well towards which my
companion and I have made a small
pilgrimage through dense hazel,
blackthorn and briar.

'Frodo country,' I say meaning, 'This is
tough going.' But we are both at ease
with the uneven path and the scratching
thorns. We even stop to admire the
liverwort *frullania* and the smouldering
lichen *degelia plumbea*. 'Smell that,' he
says and I crush it, 'Russian leather, no?'

O nature, wanting so much to share with
creatures who find it hard to stay still
– except for a few like St Fachtna who
found a fuller life in a limestone desert.

There's a *fulacht fia* close by, a four-thousand-year-old cooking and dining area used by our ancestors; the stream line running here no doubt having drawn them to this place and drawn the saint centuries later. He must have seen it as a wonderful providence to find a well and the whisper of fresh water among the stones.

Looking at the well's eye looking into mine, I'm slow to return to the world of checking what messages have arrived by satellite to the phone, that magic ring in my pocket through which I connect with people and places ghosted in from great distances but not with the unheard voices of this place pinned to the rag bush, eloquent as stone.

EARTHLY MUSIC

8:30 a.m. The buzzing of a strimmer down a summer lane is a man inadvertently scything wild flowers. At the other end of the scale is Noel Hill of an evening nursing the concertina into life, his torso still, his arms hanging loose, fingers taking direction from a tune.

Since Pythagoras, who found harmony in everything, we have been making music and asking, 'What is it? How does it take us beyond ourselves?' To the girl who strides past with earphones installed, it probably doesn't matter: 'We can tune in anywhere. We download what we like.'

Elijah sat in his cave listening for a sound he could trust. It wasn't in the roaring wind or crackling like fire but arrived as a small still voice; an image reused by Pope Francis when he says that the unfolding creation addresses us in 'a silent, paradoxical voice'.

The whine of the strimmer starts up again. Minimalist? Electronic? I close my eyes. Is there an interval there? A modulation? Listening to the soundtrack of his time, Clement of Alexandria described Jesus to his philosopher friends as the New Song, the new Orpheus who came to share with us the music of creation. We hear it in the breeze, in the strimmer, in the playing of Noel Hill.

BLOSSOM

*I*s there anything as precious as blossom? Its arrival in spring catches the deep feeling that words don't reach. The great happening that occurs with the cherry, for example, is beloved especially of the Japanese who even arrange to have picnics under its flowering branches. So, we have Bashō's tender haiku in which he catches the humour and wonder of people finding wind-blown blossom in their soup and salad.

In his poem 'From Blossoms', Li-Young Lee imagines how in eating a peach one is also eating the blossom and the shade, the fellowship and the orchard. On such days of awareness, death, he suggests, seems to lose its foothold and there is only joy and the movement 'from blossom to blossom to / impossible blossom, to sweet impossible blossom'. You can almost hear in its repetition how delightfully the word appeals to him, how it hesitates before the ecstasy it can't contain.

'Blossom' is our word for attempting to name the unnameable, a tree in flower, the divine mystery revealing itself in earth's unfolding. And we are part of it all.

The ancient ritual of bowing to another still has resonance in eastern cultures. At its core is the recognition that what is divine in me recognises the divine in you. It is one of our most fragrant gestures. When applied to the natural world, our bowing addresses the inner life of the tree – 'You are beautiful' – and is reciprocated.

TOMATO FESTIVAL

*O*ne world record may have passed us by.
That was Ireland's entry into Guinness
World Records for having the greatest
number of varieties of tomato displayed
in one place; 256 to be exact and in the
process outdoing the previous record of
241 set at Los Gatos, California, in 2017.

For most of us a tomato is just a tomato
though many people long for a 'real'
one, reckoning that taste and smell have
been engineered out of the supermarket
variety in the interest of 'travel miles' and
a longer shelf life.

Who are these people who raise so
lovingly an individual plant for its
peculiar gift of colour, size and taste?
Probably those who still believe that

difference is to be valued and preserved; people a bit like the Russian scientists who protected the vast collection of wheat seeds in the besieged city of St Petersburg (Leningrad) in 1942 and were prepared to die of starvation – fourteen of them did – rather than consume a heritage that belonged to the future. Meanwhile our ability to taste and smell atrophies together with our failure to notice the loss of abundance in our time and the dimming of the rainbow of life.

So, three cheers for the growers of tomatoes, those who call each cultivar by name much as you would a beloved companion: *Amish Gold; Sugar Plum; Virginia Sweets; Red Pear; Yellow Queen; Alexa; Black Russian.* To each of which let us answer with enthusiasm: Amen.

MIST

I wake before five and look out. Ah!
Dawn! Streetlight and headlights soon
to be written off. Minutes later I look
again and everything has withdrawn into
mist. Where did it go? How was that
done? The world at large, then the world
in hiding.

Where are we? In this sudden blooming
of mist it seems we encounter the
intangible presence of the One we call
God whose real name is written in
sycamore, granite and worm, blackbird,
heartbeat, raindrop; whose being is more
compelling as diversity than under any
single aspect.

Let us then sit down to decipher this
morning's letter and imagine the Creator

saying, 'This time for you I am mist and mist clearing. But mist not simply as a hideout for me. It is its own self, goes its own way, gracefully.'

Just as imperceptibly, through this watery milk-wash, car shapes begin to reappear as apparitions.

'Do you read me?' God is saying. 'Do you read me? Over.' We can always go to Wikipedia for help: 'Mist is a phenomenon caused by small droplets of water suspended in air. Physically, it is an example of a dispersion.'

But that kind of explanation doesn't come close to what we feel or catch our appreciation of what a delicate creature is mist, what fine threads she has, finer than the lace of the bride's veil before it is lifted by the bridegroom and their faces shine.

JOSHUA BELL

A man sat in a metro station in Washington DC one January morning and played Bach on his violin. It being rush hour, thousands hurried past. Some gave him money but couldn't stay. The ones who wanted to linger were children who had to be dragged onwards by a parent. After forty-five minutes, he had collected thirty-two dollars.

His name was Joshua Bell. Two nights earlier, the cost of seats for his concert in Boston had averaged one hundred dollars.

As an experiment, the *Washington Post* had arranged for him to play in the subway that morning in 2007. Their enquiry was: What happens to us when

we encounter beauty at an unexpected
time or place?

It would seem that we miss those notes
no matter how appealing. After all, only
six people stopped and listened for
a while then moved on. So what else
are we missing – voices, faces, tastes,
flowers, love? It may be that just because
something is not labelled special, healing
or sacred, we don't recognise it. Or we
have places to be, deadlines to meet – the
tedium and burden of it all – our phones
held close as a talisman ensuring us entry
to a world of promise and expectation.

When Joshua Bell finished playing that
morning, nobody noticed. In a Boston
theatre, following the same exquisite
piece, the audience had responded in
a frenzy of applause, had stood up to
acknowledge *beauty*.

45 / Joshua Bell

AMONG TREES

*T*oday the trees welcomed me back. I had been away a long time from their sheltering presence. Now they reached out as though they had been waiting for me. The great oaks shuffled around, the community of yew trees rubbed shoulders together, pines stood tall, imperious, the lime said, 'Come closer.'

To the non-practising tree person, this sounds sentimental. Maybe so. But when you are among trees a small bit of attention will lift the latch for you. Trees are not scenery or background but living beings; eminently sociable and learned, almost virtuous as they go about their business deep down and out of sight. We would be mesmerised if we had an inkling of all that goes on at root level as they interact with their companionable fungi. There are good friends in low places!

This morning, however, is more about gladness and peace; a peace that links us in again to the pulse of life, a gladness that invites us to stay. No need for now to name these cousins of ours: it's enough to be with them and realise that they notice our appreciative dalliance. It does them good. It does us good.

Sadly, we have lost that connection and live quite unaware that we have been tree people from the beginning, with that early memory still alive in our genes. That's what's so good about being among trees; they remind us of who we are and where we have come from; that we belong together.

LOVE STORY

*F*ungi. Like the worm, they are among
the High Kings of clay, that workaday,
underground world where life stories
begin. At first, it is their fruit bodies (what
we call mushrooms) that we see, followed
by the question, 'Are they poisonous?'

It is only recently that we have realised
the astonishing relationship between
fungus and plant, a relationship that has
been developing since the first sea weed
crept shyly onto land and began to learn
the art of being a land plant, standing
upright and trained in self-defence.

So much togetherness. Fungus and root
system. A mouth-watering symbiosis with
an endless interchange of nourishment – all
those miles of fungal threads. Mutual trust.

The great advocate for the earth, Thomas Berry says, 'To tell the story of anything, you have to tell the story of everything.' Which reminds me –

In 2011, when Leonard Cohen went to Spain to receive his Prince of Asturias lifetime achievement award he began his acceptance speech by recounting how the night before he travelled he had felt compelled to pick up his forty-year-old Spanish Conde guitar and hold it to his face. As he inhaled the fragrance of cedar as fresh as the first day he had acquired the guitar, a voice seemed to say to him, 'You are an old man and you have not said thank you; you have not brought your gratitude back to the soil from which this fragrance arose.' And, so, he says, 'I come here tonight to thank the soil and the soul of this people that has given me so much.'

It seems that when we get into gratitude there's no end to it.

COME AND HAVE BREAKFAST

*A*s I considered the spread on the breakfast table, I could only say thanks. To milk who gives herself with a splash and a child's question – did mother have a name? To the grains and seeds with their own story to tell and to tea leaves gathered in baskets from hillsides. Not to forget half a banana (the other half left for Charlie) lately of Belize or Ecuador or Cameroon.

Meals often pass us by. We just happen to be doing something else at the time, checking our phone, taking a call or making a point. Maybe to eat undisturbed on occasion might allow us a moment to consider how the sun spends every second of its existence in an outpouring of radiant light which, when processed most wonderfully by plants, is packaged for our nourishment as edible sunlight. Or to imagine that beneath the table might be heard (had we ears for it!) the sound of wind combing a field of barley, the swish of a tail or the skip of baby feet.

When I stayed for a term at An Tairseach, Dominican Farm and Ecology Centre in Wicklow, Ethna was always there to rouse us with, 'Don't disrespect the food', if ever we arrived late and unfocused for the meal over which she had presided. Because for her both kitchen and dining table were sacred spaces on which to welcome the fruits of the earth; the presence of food an invitation to communion.

EN PLEIN AIR

*T*here is something liberating about those French artists of the second half of the nineteenth century who opted to paint outdoors, forsaking the comforts of the studio with its even temperature for the opportunity to capture the play of light on water, a sudden angle of view, a gust of wind.

For those schooled in an older practice, however, this novel approach would have appeared scandalous to say the least. What was art coming to? Could these impostors be taken seriously? Yet within a generation Impressionism, as it was dismissively called, had been overtaken by newer forms of expression.

But what excitement it generated at first and still does. Perhaps its immediacy

is what appeals, or a latent desire to
be in contact with place and sky and
ordinary folk, or the sense of freshness
and freedom that it evokes. Whatever its
pleasure, I sometimes make the time to
stand in front of a lesser-known William
Stott of Oldham and his view of a
crossroads on a hilltop, *October Morning*,
to savour its mood and see what it calls
up in me.

Usually a wistfulness, a feeling of having
been a different person once, someone I
am for these moments vaguely returned
to – who I was – who perhaps I still am
but cannot sustain. Which reminds me of
Patrick Kavanagh's line, 'I do not know
what age I am', as he finds himself back
in the 'briary arms' of his home place
with the awareness, 'I cannot die / Unless
I walk outside these whitethorn hedges.'
Something like that.

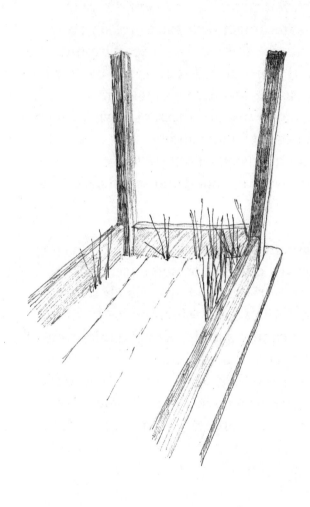

— 2 —
WHY ARE YOU PERSECUTING ME?

The trees of my childhood stand
tall in the grass
And shake their heads; what has
become of you?

Edith Södergran,
'The Trees of My Childhood'

MERMAID

I haven't forgotten Roderick Ford's
poem, 'Giuseppe', and the disturbing
episode recalled by Uncle Giuseppe, the
aquarium keeper.

In Sicily during World War Two, his
story goes, the last captive mermaid in
the world was butchered by a doctor,
a fishmonger and certain others. In
attendance also was a priest who held
one of her hands while her throat was
cut and who explained that she was 'only
a fish and fish can't speak' although she
screamed like a woman in terrible fear.
The doctor agreed with him, adding that,
'an egg is not a child' as they took the
ripe golden roe from her side, a portion
of which the priest declined.

'Starvation forgives men many things,'
Giuseppe went on, a little uncertainly,
but he could not look his nephew in the
eye. Even the soldiers expressed some
ambivalence and the creature's wedding
ring was not removed when the head
and hands were buried. Some awareness
perhaps still flickered unconsciously
in them of shared origins – how all life
began in the sea and that we have salt in
our blood – so they just reported it as a
big fish which they found on the beach
to excuse themselves and moved on.

Some time ago, an Irish newspaper
carried a photo of a woman in
Afghanistan being stoned to death in a
pit by a group of men accusing her of
adultery. And how did *they* explain it
away? Did they look her in the eye?

BIRDSONG ON THE WESTERN FRONT

*T*o the wounded soldiers on the Western Front birdsong didn't register, although it was there. With an air of detachment, the master short story writer and soldier, Saki, in his short story 'Birds on the Western Front', hands this on to us: 'In the chill, misty hour of gloom that precedes a rainy dawn … the lark would suddenly dash skyward and pour forth a song of ecstatic jubilation that sounded horribly forced and insincere', her apparent indifference to the horrors all around confirmed by the presence of a new brood tucked away among clods and shell-holes.

There were other birds, too, which he notes – kestrel, barn owl, a lone magpie (with his wry comment 'one for sorrow'), partridge and 'a wee hen-chaffinch who held her ground most likely for the sake of the young ones nesting in the battered orchard close by'. Anyone who noticed them, he adds, must have wondered how anything with wings would not have fled the scene. Saki (Hector Hugh Munro) was picked off by a sniper in 1916.

In her diary of those years, Cynthia Asquith reflects soberly on the prospect of peace: 'Will it not require more courage than what was needed before to take in the longer view again and the realisation that the dead will go on being dead.'

Passing by the upgraded Simon building on our street, I hear through an open window the voice of Lionel Richie singing, 'You're once, twice, three times a lady', spreading something like balm on an autumn evening, making up for it all. Making up. Just making it.

AIR POLLUTION

A line from Shakespeare's play, *Macbeth*, came to me when I visited friends in Co. Limerick: 'Heavenly breath smells wooingly here.' For indeed the sweetness of fresh air and spring, soil and herb made a bouquet for the nose. I had just arrived from Dublin city with its fossil-fuelled air and was beginning to wonder what I had been breathing all this time.

Months later, in another garden on the Sligo coast in the company of a robin, a fellow citizen I could work with – me with a spade, he with an eye for a juicy worm – I thought of city dwellers and commuters and of how billions of us will never get to taste anything but the world as we have built it with its toxic by-products and chemical waste.

And just as light pollution prevents us from seeing the stars and the wonder that goes with access to that vastness, so air pollution is another subtle form of deprivation, a blunting of sense, a stolen inheritance.

It is ironic that the heavenly air surrounding Macbeth's castle should contrast so sharply with the evil that lies inside where the visiting King Duncan will be murdered in his sleep. When we have sipped the nectar of pure air we should know what we have been missing. But, as happens, we forget and go back to sleep.

HOLY GROUND

I was thinking of Denis Corcoran
recently, who was an older priest
when I knew him. He took care of the
flowers and plants and loved to spend
time looking at them. 'I get a sense of
God when I am with them,' he reflected,
'but I couldn't say that too loud.' And I
remembered Mary Oliver's poem, 'Where
Does the Temple Begin, Where Does It
End?', where she admits that she never
tires of looking and inviting the world to
come closer. And it comes.

Perhaps nowhere is this awareness of
relationship better expressed than in
the letter of Chief Seattle to President
Franklin Pierce in 1854, written as a
plea and a warning to protect the land

and its creatures then being transferred
into the white man's keeping. Transferred
reluctantly, for the Chief was well
aware of the disregard of the incoming
caretakers to whom 'one portion of land
is the same as the next' for he had seen a
thousand rotting buffaloes on the prairie
shot from a passing train – a sacrilege to
those for whom the buffalo was family.

Business interests don't treat the earth
as sacred: in our time turning rain forest
to grassland for a larger beef herd and
moving indigenous people off their
land. It sounds familiar. So do the words
spoken to Moses from the burning bush,
'Take off your shoes for you are standing
on holy ground.' Where do I stand?

PEOPLE LIKE BERTA CÁCERES

*I*n his touching short story, 'The Figure on the Cross', Aidan Mathews tells of fourteen-year-old Freddie who, on regular visits to a church on his way from school, befriends the man on the cross. As their relationship grows, the boy offers to relieve his friend's distress by removing the nails pinning him to the wooden frame. The sound of dropped metal hitting marble rouses the vigilant parish priest, Fr Leo, who knows the sound of desecration when he hears it. Freddie is chased away.

The story is tantalising. It deals with suffering and innocence. It is also about the broken heart of a father, that breaks for all creatures and, in some way, suffers with them and through them; that, with a tender care, beats for the land, too, for its soils and waterways, its moon and stars – that wider community to which we belong as 'plain members and citizens' (Aldo Leopold).

This is how indigenous people relate to their home place. With a loving eye, they recognise the beauty of the world around them and are willing to lay down their lives to protect it. Like Berta Cáceres, the Honduran mother of four, assassinated in 2016 for her opposition to the building of a dam across the sacred Rio Gualcarque that would displace her people. Or the hundreds and hundreds murdered or intimidated for attempting to halt illegal land seizures for mining, logging and farming, in whose deaths the cry of the earth and of her people are one.

65 | People Like Berta Cáceres

CURIOUS CREATURES

*W*hen you come across a new
creature for the first time, it is easy
to say, 'It looks like a small pig and tastes
like chicken.' So it was for the Dutch
artist, Frans Post, who came to Brazil in
the seventeenth century to record this
amazing world. Naturally there was little
attempt to understand these creatures
in their own right; they were specimens
to be collected in a zoo and housed as a
'cabinet of curiosities'.

So, tapir and sloth and capybara, spider
monkey and green lizard were simply
curious creatures to enthral those who
saw them, comparisons with home-
grown, domestic varieties always selling
them short; jaguar, boa constrictor, giant
anteater, six-barred armadillo, exceedingly
different to the onlooker who had little

appreciation of anything about them that could link us as family.

And you might wonder: what did Frans Post think as he drew these animals in such detail, spending so much time in their company? Did he ever get a sense of presence, ever something-more-than, something deserving of admiration and respect? Who knows? Mostly, with his paintings and sketches, he was meeting the growing appetite in Europe for news of those exotic, faraway places to set the imagination racing. That people were mercilessly taken from Africa to work as slaves in the local sugar plantations hardly registered as outrageous!

Three hundred and fifty years later we are only slowly and begrudgingly granting citizenship to all species and a recognition that each one singing the hymn of its unique existence has travelled with us on a long journey; that we are kin!

FEARFULLY AND WONDERFULLY MADE

*W*hen extended to all creatures, Jesus' teaching that 'every hair on your head has been counted', reminds us that every whisker, thorn, or feather has its function and is part of an exquisite design in which the creator delights.

Fear of other creatures, however, often prevents us from knowing them – and even gives us reasons to kill. So we kill them because they are different and not like us; kill because they are in our room, in our space, in our way; kill them because we can; kill them because we have been told to, because we are afraid, because they might sting or bite; kill them because they won't speak to us.

I know the feeling, having scoured white walls in a Maltese night for the mosquito who sips my blood. In my moment of panic, her story and the majesty of her emergence escape me. I leave blood behind, hers and mine!

There is a nasty side to us: *homo homini lupus*; we fear the 'wolf' in each other. And fear can drive us to behave abominably. With fear in our eyes we don't see clearly anymore; something well expressed as 'your enemy's tears are only water'. Without empathy we see 'only water'; theirs are not real tears – not like ours!

A loving eye, on the other hand, takes a longer and a closer look; allows for the beauty in difference and celebrates it. In God's native tongue, the 'words' spoken are *scorpion, spider, worm*!

GOATS AS GARDENERS

*T*hey could hardly have known what they were doing when they removed the cover of fairy foxglove from the monastery wall or scraped up a patch of scarlet pimpernel in a corner of the car park one cloudy morning where it was dozing.

But what are we to do once we know? Hardly carry on as though nothing has happened; although for many people nothing much has happened – a few wild flowers – compared with the graver injustices humans visit on each other day after day. However, there is an attitude expressed in the phrase, 'This little bit won't matter' – insect, plastic bag, discard – that is particularly damning when you imagine it gone global and, our household, as a consequence, looking like an 'immense pile of filth' (in Pope Francis' vernacular).

In his poem, 'Musée de Beaux Arts', where Auden reflects on the fall of Icarus in Pieter Bruegel's painting, he describes how the ship sails 'calmly on', its passengers seemingly as unmoved by the sight of a boy falling out of the sky as the ploughman who may have heard the boy's cry and a splash but for whom 'it was not an important failure'!

Perhaps much of what we do is excused in this way; our negligence is small, ours are not important failures. Nevertheless, the proverb holds true: those who are faithful in small things can be trusted with greater. Or maybe James Lovelock was right and 'we are no more qualified to be stewards of the earth than are goats to be gardeners'.

ANOTHER CHRISTMAS MORNING

*T*his far West, we can mention
the word 'Rohingya' without
hesitation; a word as strange on our lips
as 'Immanuel', meaning God-with-us.
Rohingya-with-us, meaning the dispersed
families caught in a narrow strip of land
between nowhere and nowhere. Whose
are they? Are they anybody's?

Meanwhile, Mark Knopfler's 'Brothers
in Arms' is there in the background,
his poignant anti-war song with all the
sadness and regret of brother killing
brother evoked by his incomparable
playing. He can make the guitar cry.

And I remember an interview I overheard
once with the great Kerry footballer of
my youth, Mick O'Connell. To the often-

asked question, 'Mick, did you ever play
against so and so?' he liked to answer,
'No, I never did. I played with him alright
but we were on different teams.'

Behind the rustle of tearing paper and
children's voices, there is the baby light
of the world, heartbreaking as the first
floral dawn blooming for this only
earth. And always a small hand raised –
'Mama' – like the hand of Ted Hughes'
little daughter, Frieda, pointing out
'Moon! Moon!' amazed at the moon's
amazement.

The televised picture of an old man
dressed in white comes back to me. He is
banned from using the name 'Rohingya'
when he visits Myanmar because it would
identify those whom the regime would
like to disappear, give hope to those who
no longer belong.

73 | Another Christmas Morning

DORIS SALCEDO AT IMMA

*S*tanding before Doris Salcedo's visceral artistic response to the 'Disappeared' of Columbia during the 1970s, one falls quiet. Her installation, 'Acts of Mourning', bears witness to the torture, killing and humiliation of thousands of people in her country. To commemorate one nurse tortured to death and 'disappeared', she gathered up thousands of red rose petals and stitched them together to form the most delicate 'shroud' for her absent body. It flows between three rooms of the gallery as a testament of love, as a ritual of recovery.

Another installation shows a crowded space of twenty-eight tables with upturned tables placed on top and sandwiched in between a depth of earth suggesting a burial chamber or a mass grave. From the

upturned tables grow long shoots of grass
as a sign that life survives.

Dwelling on her response to the horrors of
that time evokes another extinguishing and
disappearance – that of a wealth of species
deprived of habitat and food source, and
continuously hurried out of existence by the
violence of our greed and arrogance.

Who will remember them?

The acceleration of their loss gathers pace
– from the tiny vaquita porpoise or the
Alagoas foliage-gleaner to songbirds and
insects, mammals and flowers. Perhaps, we
may take a minute's silence or wring our
hands at the latest species to make the
critically endangered list, even allow the
depth of that loss to trouble our hearts. But
what will we erect to their memory? How
will we account for their disappearance?

SWIFTS

> 'Unlike all other birds ... they never descend to the ground.'
>
> Helen Macdonald, *Vesper Flights*

'*T*here is a swift-shaped hole in my heart and it is so painful I want to weep.' This is Mary Colwell's response to the late arrival of the swifts to Bristol, her native place, and her anxiety that one year they may not come. As fewer birds sing, bees buzz, wildflowers bloom, she questions, 'Why has the tapestry of life become so threadbare?'

Thanks to James Lovelock, we now think more appropriately of Earth (Gaia) behaving as an organism, not just as a place where life happens. So it seems more than symbolic to say that earth 'grieves' for the diminishment of life in all its dazzling diversity. But we are detached from her anxiety and treat her overheating, suffocation and poisoning by innumerable chemicals as simply 'not our problem', failing to grasp that Gaia is not an *it* but an *us*.

Perhaps if she barked or made some distress call we are familiar with, we might respond but we are largely indifferent to her plight. 'Until we dare to feel how she suffers and suffer with her,' writes Pope Francis, we will not begin to understand the nature of her life-threatening illness (and ours).

If St Francis were alive today, would he not do as he did for the people of Assisi, take a hand bell and run through the streets calling, 'The swifts have returned, the swifts have returned', the skies happy again which have missed their play, their scything the air, twisting and screaming with delight?

There's a time to weep.

THE AGE OF PLASTIC

*T*he new bed arrived clad in a double layer of heavy plastic, which took ages to strip away. Printed in large letters front and back, the warning read, 'This is a dangerous product for children.'

It is now official: we are living in the age of *The Plasticene*! With 400 million tons of the stuff manufactured each year, we already have more than enough to wrap the entire planet in cling film.

And it's not going away. We all know now how dangerously long-lived it is, how whole islands of plastic junk have been created, swept up by gyres of ocean currents, how sea creatures are ingesting tiny (and not so tiny) fragments of it, how it has entered the food chain. Perhaps the child warning should be rephrased to read, 'In human hands plastic will suffocate the earth.'

Maybe this all sounds too cheerless for the online consumer whose every season is 'the season of good will'. And it's hardly fair to drag a shopper away from an imminent purchase; seems almost unnatural to separate the two. Nobody wants the party to end, even when the party is over.

Antonio Machado's question is apt: 'What have you done with the garden that was entrusted to you?' Today a child is born to a depleted and rubbished planet, short of topsoil and clean water and leaching its wondrous diversity; a child who may never see the stars.

100 ANIMALS TO SEE
BEFORE THEY DIE

*I*n Vibes and Scribes bookshop in Cork
city, I discover *100 Animals to See Before
They Die*. A catchy title, I say to myself, as
I open at random on the dark face of the
bonobo; one of our own, with 95 per cent
of shared genetic material and a gift for
community living. Still it's hard for us to
believe with St Francis that this creature,
our unclaimed cousin, reflects an aspect
of divine goodness and has a message to
convey to us.

On a different scale, hundreds of 'small'
languages are easing into silence, taking
their treasure hoard of perception and
response with them. Will they hover in a
museum or in 'The Laboratory of Exotic
Sounds' together with recordings of bird
and animal speech of creatures gone

extinct? The voice of empire bellows and the little ones go quiet!

But from the beginning, life has evolved in a dazzling kaleidoscope of expression. Our different ways of being here are evidence of that; we and every other creature, all making our acclaim in our own way, 'It's good to be here.'

And what of earth's 'groaning', the sound that Paul interpreted poetically as labour pains (as creation being born again), but which in our time we hear as protest, accusation and grief? What kind of species turns on its mother, poisons its food supply and pollutes the living stream? Homo sapiens signs off, fells a forest, lays waste a homeland: *let us consume, consume, consume.*

ROAD KILL

*D*riving along, I notice a dead body by the roadside. No one has stopped. Could it be that no one has noticed? True, it doesn't look like anyone we know wrapped up in a fur coat but it has the signs of a hit and run.

The adult badger did not go home last night. Impossible to think that he was not missed. Convenient to say that badgers spread disease and don't feel like we do. Of course, we could equally say that we don't feel like they do.

In my passing glance he looked thrown there without a second thought as though life did not once flow as knowingly through his whole being as through ours. It occurred to me that few tears, if any, would be shed for a neighbour who lived locally, had raised a family, learnt to survive with a unique intelligence and praised God in his own way. Yet no Good Samaritan might be expected to stop to check his wounds or say a prayer. The Road Safety Authority would not be informed.

Just so, in an Australian bushfire where the commentary is exclusively on the human toll, Jean O'Brien reminds us of the tragedy of other lives, 'Flying foxes swaddled inside their coat of leather wings swelter, / baby marsupials boil in their mother's pockets', together with a multitude of fellow creatures we think don't count. Can we survive this soul loss?

CEMENTING THE GARDEN

*T*he time came when we wanted to cement over our gardens, to bury them, to make parking space for cars and a surface resistant to rain. We forgot what it means to have a garden with memories embroidered in plant and bush, where children tumble in summer. Even if only grass grew there, it was a living space, home to a host of creatures; worms farmed the soil.

We had a garden once, so the story goes, but we banished ourselves from it. No god ordered us out. We had our own reasons for leaving! Which helps to explain why we need seed banks now to save, store and propagate the precious varieties that remain.

To be a seed saver is a holy occupation. 'This seed is potent as the seed / Of knowledge in the Hebrew Book,' wrote Patrick Kavanagh, as he gathered intuitively that seed is creation's storehouse and strategy. It is the journey from being dead and buried to blossom, flower and fruit; and earth a womb where seed comes alive and magic happens – roses and rhubarb, sweet potato, lettuce, sweet pea.

Having cut our roots, however, we don't know how poor we are, we who have technologised our lives beyond recognition, built underground tunnels to carry our exuberant traffic, forgotten our place, forgotten our name – Adam – one who has sprouted from the earth. We were gardeners once …

MUSICAL PARENTS

J was sitting down to write when a
loud bang on the glass door startled
me. I turned to see a blackbird flying off.
She landed on the fence, preened herself,
and then flew off to other adventures.

It was a wake-up call. At such times, what
can you say about creation other than
point to the garden birds playing in the
willow arch and to the wind running
through grass?

Yesterday evening, my friend Caroline
showed us the bat she had brought
home from an office into which the
little creature had entered by mistake.
A distraught secretary, on finding the
dead body on the back of her chair, had
screamed, ran out the door and rang

the Wildlife Service. She would not be
returning, she made clear, until that
awful *thing* had been removed.

It was a *common pipistrelle*, Caroline said,
as she held out the small, frozen body for
us to see. Of course he had a name, she
said, and a story and musical parents and
amazing abilities like 'seeing' in the dark,
but being young, had lost his way.

We have a long way to go when it comes to
appreciating the astonishing lives of other
creatures. And further, in granting that any
interaction with them can be a moment
of grace, a chance encounter with fur and
feather in which 'I' becomes 'we'.

This morning Caroline's text reads,
'The family I visited last night had five
hundred *soprano pipistrelles* in their attic.
Now that's what I call a bat roost!'

87 | Musical Parents

UNHEARD MELODY

*W*hen Sinead Stone finished singing 'The Prayer', the wedding company broke out in applause. It was her voice and something to do with the way she became the song that beguiled us. 'Born to sing, she was,' someone was overheard to say when our busy hands came to rest.

The great Donegal fiddler, John Doherty, is remembered by his friends withdrawing into himself to listen to a recording of pipe music while convalescing in a nursing home. They recalled that 'his eyes looked only inward' as the music carried him away.

It appears there is an unheard melody that runs like a thread through every living thing. When we connect with it, as we do when we are moved by its embodiment in a tune or a voice, we, too, are carried away. It is never simply about a polished performance but happens when a singer or musician has tapped into the spring of himself or herself.

Like a diviner, Sinead points us to where the underground stream is flowing, where refreshment is to be found: 'Lead us to a place, guide us with your grace' and I sense the truth of it like a breath on the back of my neck.

In 1917, near Ypres in Belgium, Francis Ledwidge heard the robin's song from a broken tree and heard in it the little fields around Slane calling to him. That was shortly before a shell exploded beside him while on a tea break from road-making. But he had made the connection.

UNLESS YOU BECOME LIKE LITTLE CHILDREN

I wish for you a world
where the green hairstreak may rest
upon your unhurting hand

John Feehan,
'Two Poems for Ann'

EARTH CHILD

It seems as if the whole world is destined to live in cities. But perhaps it is only someone who has spent time in the countryside and been 'tamed' by it, who is left with that longing to return to some place where something wonderful happened to her or him while gazing into a field or listening to the sound of leaves full of themselves; to the wood pigeon naming the unnameable or cattle shuffling behind a hedge.

Maybe you want to get back to that stream you discovered once and kept as a secret hideaway where you learnt to read the flowing script of the currents chuckling around the stones, which you could understand because it was intended for you.

So much so that after the holidays you
returned at a loss to your family, to the
school playground and the raised kerb
that separates the safe path from the
busy road. In your child's world there
were no paths. You made them. Where
you went the way opened for you. Later
you realise what you still miss: the stream
with its shared freedom, the coolness of
its flow, its playful fingers forever inviting
yours.

And you want to go home as deeply
as anyone displaced – wherever home
may be. And what is it that draws you
now but an echo of an echo. Your ears
are burning. There is talk of you: 'Has
anybody seen the child who used to
come here?'

FRANKIE

*M*y friend, Paddy Griffin, has sent me a forty-second video of his two-week-old grandson. I realise it is the eve of the Feast of the Epiphany, the twelfth day of Christmas by which time the long-haul travellers will have arrived at a manger in Bethlehem.

It strikes me now that these people were not necessarily wise to start with but wised-up as they made their journey. Indeed, it seems likely that they came into true wisdom upon seeing the baby in a derelict place among animals and animal smells.

For it is the baby who is wise in his wonder, coming to terms with being outside his mother's cosy body in a first

knowing that puts to shame what we
call wise, and with a frailty that humbles
what we consider strong.

In this setting, to become wise is to
be dazzled by unconditional love as
the baby looks at you with the eyes of
God and you are restored to your first
innocence as the beloved child you are.

When moments of infancy are revealed
to us in creation as sunrise, snowdrop,
larva or lamb, are we not also returned
to a forgotten way of seeing, our eyes
refreshed as when we emerge from time
spent in an art gallery to a world of
vibrant colour, a world washed clean of
all our craving?

'MY DADDY IS WEIRD'

*T*he story behind 'The Fairies'
Hornpipe', according to the piper
and folklorist, Séamus Ennis, is as
follows.

A man going home late from a wedding
loses his way but remembers in a lucid
moment the cure for being lost: you take
off your coat, turn it inside out then put
it on again. He does so and finds himself
not three fields from his house where a
fairy host is dancing to music played by a
piper. Telling the story to his disbelieving
neighbours the next morning, he plays
the fairy tune for them as irrefutable
proof of his adventure.

I can almost hear Séamus's corncrake
voice as he revels in the mischief of

the story's twists and turns with the merriment of a born storyteller who draws out each coloured thread as he leads the listeners spellbound into another world.

In Listowel, many years ago, the poet, Michael Hartnett shared this intimacy with us. In the local primary school, children were being asked by the teacher what their father did for a living. 'My Daddy is weird,' Michael's son had said, a description of himself that Michael relished, overhearing all the strangeness and waywardness that the word inferred.

There is something weird in the sound of uilleann pipes that could turn you inside out if you let it, could lead you astray. That's when you might remember to take off your coat, turn it inside out and put it on again.

Then you're right as rain.

WATCH ME

*A*s a close observer of our foibles and false steps, Jean-Jacques Sempé, the famous French illustrator, offers rueful commentary in his cartoons on the way we live our hit-and-miss lives. 'Will you just look at us!' they imply. One that I often recall has a baby enter a room in which his parents are watching TV. 'I'm walking,' he announces, obviously startled to find himself an upright, mobile human for the first time. His preoccupied parents, however, don't turn around and this life-changing moment for their darling son passes them by.

Much like the father in Harry Chapin's song, 'Cat's in the Cradle', who misses out on his boy's growing up because 'there were planes to catch and bills to pay'.

The poignant chorus offsets the child's loaded question, 'When you coming home, Dad?' with the dismissive reply, 'I don't know when but we'll get together then, you know we'll have a good time then.' The twist, of course, is that the boy will turn out to be just like his father, with no time to spend with Dad, who now has all the time in the world – or what he's left of it.

A child, like a plant, needs time and attention and an approving word to thrive. 'Don't forget to give a drink of water to the plants and say hello while I'm away,' I say to my friend, extending Don Bosco's advice: 'They must know you believe in them, they must know they are loved.'

A PAIL OF WATER

*W*hen you see a child lost in attention while holding her hands under running water you sense that some deep connection is being made beyond words. Through enjoying the feel of it – cool, silky and playful – she is having a spiritual experience although it's not the usual way to describe it: 'Turn off that tap, will you!'

It is no coincidence that almost every form of religious expression makes use of water – from submersion in a sacred river as a form of renewal, to dipping one's fingers in a font by a church door, to a minister sprinkling drops of water over the people in blessing.

Like life itself, however, we savour it best in small amounts, in a cup of water

when we are thirsty or being hooked
up to a drip in a hospital when we are
dehydrated. It seems we find it hard to
comprehend abundance.

Where water is piped to our homes, for
instance, it soon becomes simply 'what
comes out of the tap', just as an ocean can
be reduced to 'where fish live' and 'where
we bury our waste'! We fail to appreciate
its living quality since no Grace is
regularly said before taking a sip (or a
dip), no gratitude addressed to the source.

When Anne Sullivan held Helen Keller's
hand under the water pump and traced
the word *water* on her other hand, the
blind, deaf and mute girl understood.
We need to make that discovery again, to
reverence water for what it is, or *who* she
is, according to St Francis, 'Sister Water,
humble, precious, and pure.'

THE REASON I JUMP

*T*hirteen-year-old Naoki Higashida tells this story:

Having lost the earlier contest, Hare wants a rematch. Tortoise, as reigning champion, at last concedes. The animals gather. At the gun, Hare streaks away. Tortoise pumped up with adrenalin, trips over something and ends up on his back. The animals carry him home. Later, when Hare crosses the line, punching the air, there is nobody there to cheer.

In *The Reason I Jump*, Naoki allows us access to the hypersensitive world of someone considered slow and uncommunicative. With remarkable insight, he gives us a glimpse into autism with its fears and uncertainties. Time, for example, he says, is 'as difficult for us to grasp as picturing a country we've never

been to. ... Exactly what the next moment
has in store for us never stops being a
big, big worry.'

No wonder he writes of his longing to go
back to a 'distant, distant, watery past'
before the first life forms emerged onto
dry land, before our ancestors discovered
time.

Even when ignored or pushed away, he
finds solace and friendship in nature from
whom 'we receive a sort of permission
to be alive in this world and our entire
bodies get recharged ... Nature will always
give us a great big hug here in our hearts.'
Just by looking at nature, he says, he can
feel swallowed up into it, a sensation so
amazing 'I forget that I'm a human being
and one with special needs as well'.

'And the black crow looked no less perfect
against the deep blue than the white dove.'

PLANET DANCING

*A*ccording to Hafiz, the Sufi mystic,
God knows only four words and
keeps repeating them: 'Come dance with
me.' The invitation written in our genes
and coming from the great Mover and
Shaker whose nature is dance, who sets
the universe dancing.

So Earth spins as it goes on its annual
journey around the sun, our parent
star (something impossible to believe
while we held earth to be the centre of
everything). And stars must feel for their
planets and sense the allure of other
stars and galaxies, all choreographed to
dance in space time.

The whirling dervishes of the Sufis
understand something of this, for they

twirl and wheel to express their ecstatic
communion with the Divine who is
dancing in them. Most of us, however, opt
for a more static God who moves rather
stiffly and is not much fun. By contrast,
one of the earliest images we have of the
divine is of a threesome dancing together
with heaven and earth an extension of
that original ballet.

A dancing world makes sense to us,
confirming our place in the cosmic flow.
One day a parliament will stand up
before the order of business and begin to
sway together, moving as one body. And
a praying congregation begin to dance,
having 'got it' at last, that God is the
dancer, creation the dance as we fall into
step with every other dancing life form,
from hydra to hippo!

SUCH COMPANY

I was going to tell you about my dog but
I hesitate. He's getting on and doesn't
move about without me; doesn't even
bark. We're friends from childhood when
he would always sleep on my pillow. His
eyesight is bad now and stitching marks
an old injury; his once fawn coat is
threadbare—

Just then a blast of light shines in and
spots the face of the clown who watches
over me. And suddenly I am looking
into his lit-up face and seeing something
like sadness there despite his bright,
red circle of nose and elongated smile,
his blue eyes, orange hair, his jumpsuit
multicoloured and shiny.

In boots too big for him, he stands to attention and stares intently towards me until I turn a little key in the middle of his back. That's when he starts to dance, moving his body to the music that rises from inside him. It is that simple! I turn the key; he sways and bows, dips and stretches for as long as the melody lasts.

I hadn't always thought of him like that; saw him more as a plaything, a toy, a souvenir until today when he reveals something else. In that catch of sunlight I see myself for a moment poised, on the edge, waiting for the music to begin. It begins and we move together, matching each other, turning this way and that. Then, as suddenly, it stops and we return to our old selves, enlivened, connected, somehow changed.

THREE LITTLE PIGS

We are often reminded that we live in a flimsy house built of thoughts, which is not the kind of place you'd choose to spend your whole life! What with the shifting, drifting nature of thinking, it's hard to get a foothold or feel at home.

In a house made of thoughts, the bricks are paper-thin, the roof forever in a state of disrepair as one image replaces another. There are no windows and no skylight full of stars. Which reminds me of the three little pigs building their house of straw. And how the wolf came: 'He huffed and he puffed and he blew the house down.'

Despite ourselves, we can live a lifetime in our prison-house of thoughts – of grudges, fears, worries, regrets – and miss out on the fresh air of the ever-present moment. When we mistake our thoughts for the real thing, we just go on rebuilding with the same old materials – unlike the little pigs!

That is until we wake up and see beyond these habitual thoughts with all their advice and scolding. It is then that we open up and step outside to a real world awaiting our precious attention. Breathe.

It's summer. Look at a bush full of bees on a nectar trip, hear a bird speaking out and feel the breeze on your face. The world is addressing you as friend. Come out to play, it says. Wise up, will you.

Breathe.

JASMINE

*M*y friend is part of a music and dance routine celebrating Chinese New Year. Standing there in the crowd, I feel a little dowdy and out of place among the reds and yellows of oriental jubilee. Furthermore, I have just been introduced to the game of Chinese chess by a girl who recognises in me a slow learner, though I love the idea of a river flowing across the board. Suddenly, the distinctive sound of the guzheng or Chinese zither wakens me and I am tempted to imagine myself as a young Chinese musician learning the melody of 'Plum Blossom in Three Movements' or 'Evening Song from the Fishing Boat'.

We watch the festival film, *Up the Yangtze*, with its notes of subtle commentary as it tells the story of Yu Shui who leaves home to work on the cruise ships that travel the great river and of her family who must also leave because of the rising waters following the construction of the Three Gorges Dam, the largest hydroelectric project on earth. The relocation of the poor is a small matter in a country's progress!

Back in the hall, the ceremonial lion is rampaging through the crowd with a cymbal and drum accompaniment. The writers of calligraphy are launching a brush as I pick up a book by Ping Fu, open it at random and read, 'I believe that behind every closed door is an open space.'

A RIBBON FOR BRIGID

'*I*t's instinctive,' Teresa says. 'You feel it in your blood. Earth stirs, shoots appear.' She's talking about Brigid and the sense of her embodiment in the full-bellied life-fest of spring.

Goddess and national saint, girl and mother in a monastery garden, not meek and mild but shrewd and savvy. Seer and overseer, she gives protection to entrances and stepping stones, to poets and blacksmiths, animals and land.

She is neither to be contained in a monastery nor corralled by the state, this mystic of the natural world whom we celebrate in the ancient practice of weaving a sun-cross of rushes. By doing so, we are weaving together in her

name all strands of wisdom from death-
resurrection to the rhythm of seasons on
our sun-shocked earth.

I call up Elizabeth for guidance. She
describes how she celebrates the ritual
for Brigid's eve. At dusk, she leaves a
length of ribbon outside so that as Brigid
passes in the dewfall she will bless it.
Afterwards, it will be cut into pieces and
shared with neighbours who can apply
the healing fabric to a body's pain.

Imbolg, February 1st, is the day we invite
her wise and wholesome presence into
our lives. For those of us who have lived
at a distance from the earth, it is still
not too late to find our way home again
in the company of Brigid as we take her
hand and go play like children beneath
the weeping birch where clumps of
snowdrops shed their light.

113 | A Ribbon for Brigid

DEAD FOX

*F*rom two storeys up it looked unclear
so I called someone to the window
and asked, 'Could it be?' Without
hesitation, he concurred. So now we had
a dead fox in our yard even as a live one
nosed among the stones for a scent or a
half-scent.

I told others, 'We have a dead fox in the
yard but it looks as if the legs have been
tied together.' As I considered it, the tail
didn't look quite right unless a burning
had crinkled it into strands. The colour,
too, was faded, even … singed?

Next day, considering should we have
the body removed, I rang my colleague,
Bridie. She looked out her window and
then called Stephen. Peering through

the railings from the ground floor, he confirmed it was nothing more than a piece of scrap from a burnt-out car! The fox had disappeared and the story too.

It was a joke for a while with Stephen asking, 'Are you sure it's not a seal?' for he was too polite to say, 'Would you not think of going to Specsavers?'

I thought of that line: 'We see things not as they are but as we are' and wondered what it would take to reverse that bias.

This evening we are at the window again watching our resident fox slipping from shadow to shadow, bringing news from town of occasional treats and regular letdowns.

WORDS IN THEIR JACKETS

*H*ow amazing is that; our ability to take experience, find its register then see it metamorphose as language squirming across the page? How is it done? Today there is neuroscience to lend a hand but it doesn't seem to capture the magic of that seamless flow from outside to in and from inside to out again dawning as insight, wonder, pain or loss.

Perhaps you remember the shock of hearing the first words your child uttered, linking the word 'apple' with the shiny green sphere on the table or the word 'sweet' with that tasty delight hiding in a wrapper. Or how she responded to 'here take my hand' as two hands fell in together.

Later we learn what can't be said, only
pointed at – over there, beyond, further.
Words going all shy, doubling back on
themselves into a whisper before all that
can't find expression – geese flying, the
perfection of a spider's web, love light, the
sound of a horse-drawn hearse ...

Or when you emerge some morning to
discover that the sky has peeled off to
reveal an exquisite blue and the world
looks lit up from within; early blossom
a reason to cheer and children running
ahead of their buggies. At such moments
the tired words all fall down. They're not
up to it. *Just let it be*, you find yourself
saying, *let it speak for itself* as you drop your
guard and hand yourself over to whatever
it is that makes it so.

ALICE AT FIVE

*A*lice at five has been to see a small
farm. She has been greatly taken
by the sow and how one ear falls across
her eye. 'Does she eat mud? What is that
smell?' And then she tells how the sow
tried to kiss her. She finds that so funny.

Sweet and sour go hand in hand in
another world where 'the lamb will
lie down with the wolf' and the sow
bestow a kiss on the cheek of a little girl.
What are we to make of it all? All this
difference appreciated for its just being
different, the whole unsteady whoosh of
it captured in Louis MacNeice's words
as, 'The drunkenness of things being
various.'

The truth is that fulfilment belongs to
every creature irrespective of species.
Maybe the sow did not want to kiss
Alice but what struck me was how she
sensed immediately some kind of kinship
despite the obvious difference and the
smell!

As adults, we can lose that closeness and
the sensitivity to appreciate that each
creature reflects something of God and
has a wisdom to share with us; that each
creature gives praise by its very existence.

To refuse to consider, then, how animals
are reared in a modern food-production
system is to live in denial – until the day
we have the courage to ask, how is the
killing done? Did the animal imprisoned
in this cramped space ever truly live?

ALL SLEEPING THINGS

*T*hough I mark out a territory and call it 'mine' there are other creatures that also call it home and raise their families there. They know the local scene and have a favourite place from which to view the world; hence, all the nest building, burrowing and looking for a hideout to winter in.

Take a hedgehog, for instance, who can ramble up to two kilometres at night, the one Peter found inside his back door recently. His first thought was that it had snuck in for a little warmth as the door was open; then climbed onto the dog's sofa, curled up and went to sleep. Later he had to concede it had to be Mack, his springer, who had carried in the spiky ball from the garden and placed it there.

Generally we are ignorant of the lives
of other creatures, despite our common
ancestry. So even a fly in a room can
lead to consternation and imaginings
of plague or simply 'disease'. Or a
wasp in autumn, who has good reason
for drawing attention to itself; being
homeless, hungry and 'all over the place'.

It seems we are biodiverse-averse and
find it difficult to believe that a creator
could make a buzzing sound or wear a
crown of thorns. When divine goodness
is revealed in the life of another creature,
it is as if we are invited to replace the
possessive 'mine' with the inclusive 'ours'.
'All sleeping things are children,' writes
Jenny George in 'The Sleeping Pig' –
hedgehog, refugee and pig.

THE UNSEEABLE
ANIMAL

I love the childlike hope of Wendell
Berry's daughter expressed in his
poem, 'To the Unseeable Animal', that
somewhere in the world is an animal
that will forever elude capture in the nets
of our knowing; that can safely go on
playing out its life un-endangered by us,
un-entered in our catalogues, our dead
museums, our compounds.

'You don't need to throw a stone at
him,' Matt Talbot said to a young Paddy
Laird, who had called in to see him on
his lunch break, although the rat was on
the table nibbling at Matt's bit of dried
bread. When recalling this incident later,
Paddy told how the saintly man 'spoke
to the rat, nice and soft like, "Come on,
now, get down", and the rat obeyed'. And

how he then explained that rats were God's creatures too and had their job cleaning the sewers just as he had his in the timber yard.

Speak well of all creatures. Treat them well. A tall order for most of us. But maybe that's what being holy is – growing to appreciate divine purpose in everything.

To be wrong about animals is to be wrong about God, wrote Thomas Aquinas, suggesting that with clear sight we might recognise that every animal is in some sense *unseeable* as each one expresses something of the Great Unseen.

NAUGHTY FACE

*T*here is the donkey who appears to our imagination in a Bethlehem stable and the one who walks in the Jerusalem parade amid cheering fans. And another placed centre stage in a painting by Orazio Gentileschi, whose large head looking over the exhausted family as they rest on their way to Egypt – baby suckling and Joseph stretched out on the ground – could be thinking, 'Who remembers the one who carries them?'

To a Father who notices the fall of a sparrow, the ass is more than 'a dumb beast'. He, too, is loved into existence in some way with every other creature, including those we lord it over, oblivious of how in our keeping they are often mistreated and misunderstood.

Time to Call Home / *124*

In contrast there's the story of Elisabeth Svendsen. Little did she know when in 1969 she decided to buy a donkey named Naughty Face that her heart would be blown open by seeing other neglected donkeys for sale; that she would found a worldwide sanctuary movement to care for thousands more just like them; and found a Trust that would create opportunities for children with special needs to bond with these loving friends.

And there's Brian, who, after his awful accident, liked nothing better than to drive down in his chair to sit and gaze and talk to his two donkeys, Tess and Bess; his affinity with them deepened perhaps by his own sense of confinement and their still and attentive presence. They understood.

— 4 —
CALLING HOME

The earth said
remember me.
The earth said
don't let go.

Jorie Graham, 'Poem'

AN AFTERTASTE

'Supper' seems to be yet another word on its way out; going, going ... With that remark, I am no less dating myself as I recall my grandfather warming a cup of milk to take the chill off it, then drinking it with a plain biscuit or two before bedtime. Of course, that was when the accepted order ran: breakfast, dinner, tea and supper.

I was moved in this direction when I stumbled upon an evocative sentence from a letter written by Emily Dickinson to her dear friend, Elizabeth Holland in 1866, which reads, 'The supper of the heart is when the guest has gone.' In a preceding line, she had written, 'When you went the love came. I supposed it would', implying that the memory of friends having spent time together survives with a delightful aftertaste, as a small repast.

It reminded me, then, of the early disciples breaking bread together and how they understood it as a 'supper of the heart', a sustaining memory; the friend has gone but what was understood so deeply by his farewell gesture continues to nourish them.

And there are places, too, that nourish you long afterwards because of an encounter you have had; there was that slant of hill, a huddle of trees, a stretch of stream where something spoke to your heart once and ever after, or that time when a street fox crossed your path. Whatever the special place, the memory of that experience can still warm and fill you with a longing like the longing to go home.

AS THE POSTMAN SAID

*A*llow me to speak up for snail mail!
For snail is not so slow and these
little creatures with a shell know well
their whereabouts and will accomplish
all that's asked of them from life with
due diligence and wisdom. Even an
hour or two spent in their company, you
suspect, would be awesome.

I received a letter yesterday (not an
email) that I have read more than once
and will return to. My friend has taken
the time. For as long as she wrote I
guess she was thinking of me, of shared
interests, some local news, mentioning
how the journey is going, the sick and the
mended, before signing off.

And recently Maurice came across some letters in a book of my grandfather's. They read like relics of another age now, like the following one from April 1960 with its formality of expression and comforting tone that sounds quaint to us: 'Hereabouts the weather is seemingly settled and seasonable and that is as one wants it in relation to things generally.' Sixty years later, I say, bring back letter writing. Don't let the postal service die! Leave something for the next generation!

'I don't give gifts anymore,' says Rupert Sheldrake. 'I give experiences,' as he tells of going on a walking pilgrimage to Canterbury with his grandson to mark the young man's birthday. A letter is a little pilgrimage from one heart to another, a Camino made by the hand as it moves deliberately down the page.

SOIL MATES

'I feel such a peace puttering around in the dirt with all the wiggly, slimy, ugly little creatures.'

Maura 'Soshin' O'Halloran

*S*eamus Heaney's 'Digging' is one of his best-known poems. It arises from a memory of his father digging and imagines how that hands-on activity is somehow shared between father and son, one using a spade, the other finding a way into the soft mulch of language with a pen.

To use a spade with any facility is probably beyond most of us now, but more regrettable is our steady retreat from the earth and any appreciation of its moods and seasons.

Happily, I can still remember my father opening a leafy drill in our back garden to

uncover a hide of potatoes, which we
gathered up for dinner, light-headed with
the earth smells released from his digging.

When the old people go they often take
their skills with them; in this case, how
to sustain a family from a patch of earth,
how to prepare the ground, nourish it,
how to plant seeds. These days we entrust
ourselves to the supermarket and to the
hope that the packaged food will arrive
on time from wherever it comes while we
push away the thought of a failed delivery
and the nightmare of empty shelves.

Seamus Heaney was well aware of our need
to be connected to the earth and all his life
drew nourishment from his home place.
We would be foolish to think we can so
easily sever our roots for a virtual life and
outsourced food. Earthling *Adam* needs
adamah (the earth) as a dipper needs a
running stream, as a child needs play.

GOING

*T*he sales pitch of a well-known brand
insists, 'When things are gone, they're
definitely gone', which is certainly true
when applied to the extinction of a
species, say, or the palpable loss of life's
abundance. It seems that what we would
like to ditch, dump, bury – chemicals,
toxins, nuclear waste – stays around for
a very long time while the departure of
what we cherish seems in hindsight to
have slipped away while our heads were
turned.

Someone wants to buy us a better version
to replace the old and, before we know
it, we have thrown out the oil lamps,
the solemn-faced clock, a rusty hacksaw,
sewing machine, armchair, cobbler's
last, tongs and hat stand together with

the values that went with them: long companioning with a garment, manual skills and the wit of living comfortably with enough.

There's 'a rapture in deserted things', muses Michael Coady, as he considers the 'lush forgotten sidings of country railway stations'. A bit like my father who had an eye for the possibilities hidden in what was thrown away; the shiny back of a small electric fire, for instance, that he spent days trying to incorporate into his old lawnmower then adding a green plastic box to the rear. Though nothing fancy, he pushed his new-look machine up and down the lawn all summer long with a quiet satisfaction. Then he was gone.

CACTUS

For the last week or so I have been watching our cactus plant coming into flower. Now in warm surroundings it unfolds in a crown of blossom. Each flower head in its light pink attire peels back to reveal a stigma with a purple tip and the stamens laden with pollen, a reminder to us that the plant is expecting 'someone'; that it has its own business to attend to, its own way of praising in a form of 'worship' unique to itself.

For many months the cactus had presented itself as a dark green plant, a bit dusty, hardly worth a second glance, its lifestyle essentially inward; then this sudden flowering. We would never have imagined it was capable of this transformation, this exuberance. But there it is.

To watch our loved ones die is not easy and their going from us buffets our hearts terribly; their absence gnaws at our being. Yet in this floral metaphor there is a comfort, a sign for hard times which says that, though beyond our imagining, those who have died are now showing off their inner structure and delicate colour – their soul like a leaping flame.

We honour them in their flowering and finery, in their vigour and ecstasy. One day we, too, must make that crossing. In those hours may we recognise a familiar voice and may the burden of our dying be light.

THE STORY GOES

*T*hey had everything – peace, food, love, laughter. Then one day, it is reported, they had an idea. Surely there had to be more to it than this. If it was so good here then it must be even better further on.

Disregarding the suspect logic, they began to listen in to the hiss in *surpass, impress, success* and longed to be somewhere else. 'We can do better,' they whispered to each other. 'Let's go taste it for ourselves.' They did and found it very good.

The gardener was surprised the evening he came by and found them missing. They were still bodily there, of course, but in their heads they had moved on –

Time to Call Home / 138

no more silly games of hide and seek
for them or long walks and chats with
the gardener who pruned the fruit trees.
They wanted more.

Serpentine knowledge has this quality,
however. It involves us in coils of
thinking so labyrinthine, in the end we
don't really know where we are. We line
our pockets with uncertainty, suspicion
and discontent.

The story is about us, about how we
leave the present moment in search
of something better; that is, the next
moment, the one we will as readily leave
for the succeeding one, not realising
that the present is always the doorway
to paradise if we can only enter it, look
around and name the plants and animals
– such blessings!

'HAVE YOU CAUGHT ANYTHING?'

The Drowse pulsed like a living thing, its waters dark and sinewy. It was a good fishing river, judging by the number of cars and their county registrations. Scattered along its banks were the fishermen, in waders, casting. With a flick of the wrist, a line sang through the air, and dropped halfway across. Occasionally, a salmon heading upstream would make a splash as he leaped for a fly. In that serene setting, few words, if any, were said. The men (mostly) were happy just being there, in tune with the river. They moved like people in a trance, following some inner prompting; appeared as monks silently pursuing an ordinary task for its hidden meaning.

I was impressed and a little envious. And yet I had seen that attention before in a person gardening, in a farmer's eyes, in a woman in a clothes' shop feeling the fabric, in a child at play, in the shake of hands lighting a candle.

These are the moments we lose our self-consciousness and forget the many 'shoulds' and 'oughts' that have accumulated over years; when it feels as if our whole being, mind and heart, is moving in the same direction; as if *success* and *failure* didn't exist – as if that distinction had never been made.

Such moments of unfolding (or enfolding) are outside time, as when you notice that the pot plant you are tending is attending to you or, for the person fishing, the feeling of being at one with the river and the river voices.

PRAYER PLANT

I go into our small chapel at dusk and
find the plant praying, its leaves raised
in salute, perhaps its way of listening. I
cannot hope to understand the prayer
life of my Red Herring-bone plant,
Maranta tricolor, and can only surmise.
I know for certain it is beautifully and
wondrously alive; the red veins in the
leaves striking against a light and a
darker green; the undersides a purple red.

Of course the plant is in love with
light and knows east from west. I am
reminded that it is made with the same
loving care as I am. Even when carelessly
left thirsty, it seems never to give up on
its desire to praise.

Most people never consciously pray with
a plant nor do they understand how
deeply our fellowship matters; how close
we are, how far back we go.

Sometimes when I can't pray myself I can
always say to the Red Herring-bone plant,
'Pray for me.' And I know it will, not just
pray for my need, but pray in my stead!
In other words, represent me before the
Joy of the Universe and make it plain
that we are here – both of us – and that
our answer is *yes*.

In return, I test the soil with a finger
and pour a little water for my friend, this
messenger sent ahead of us to prepare
the way, to arrange the welcome.

CONSUELA

'Meet Consuela,' John says and solemnly introduces us. A Chilean rose tarantula actually, large enough to fit in my palm. I am a little tentative as I receive the gift of this creature and place my hand over the table in case I suddenly withdraw it and she falls to the floor.

She has come from South America but is not just for show. She will be well minded and indeed on my next visit I can see the wonder growing in my friend's eyes. He is as attentive to her as a child to a kitten. 'Made with the same loving care as we are,' he says as he highlights her stillness, her living presence, feeding habits, the mystery of her.

'Does she sigh?' I consider out loud, 'So far from home.' 'Yes and no,' he says, 'but not like us.' Then tells me how one sunny day he had brought her out to the garden and returned to find her missing from her box. As he headed back downcast towards the house, suddenly there she was near the back door. 'She could have gone a hundred ways,' he said. 'Why this one?' Perhaps she may have had more on him than he knew as she followed him home.

'Something godlike about her,' I ventured, after she died, knowing he wouldn't misunderstand.

'But not as humans know godlike as a reflection of themselves,' he added. He missed her for a long time afterwards. In fact, misses her still.

145 / *Consuela*

LET THERE BE LIGHT

*T*his morning I am up in time to see
first light creeping over tall buildings
and spreading across the sky. I am
reminded of Luke's consoling image of
God's loving kindness coming to visit us
'like the dawn from on high'.

For the nine days before Christmas, this
expectation and longing is summed
up in our prayer by the word 'O'. At the
winter solstice, for instance, we say, 'O
rising Sun. O come and enlighten those
who sit in darkness and in the shadow of
death.'

This vowel is so expressive of us. It
can stretch from the anguished 'O' of
Munch's iconic figure crossing the Oslo
bridge to the 'O' of hushed wonder

on the face of a child; from the 'O' of the Advent prayer, which at evening introduces our dearest wish, 'O please do come', to the heartache of the lonely person who calls someone for no reason or asks, 'Can't you stay awhile?' as she's tired of shadows.

This long tradition of yearning is as urgent as ever as we press our concern for our endangered earth in this way: 'O Wisdom, you come forth from the mouth of the Most High. You fill the universe and hold all things together in a strong yet gentle manner. O come to teach us the way of truth.' A hope we share with those who set their passage graves in the Boyne Valley to face the rising sun.

WILD GARLIC

With the loss of some parkland to a new road, we are temporarily missing the wooden Madonna that stood among the trees. She is still essentially tree but in the sculptor's hands has become a figure of inwardness and slow time.

'Inwardness', like 'woodland', is one of those comforting words, easy in the mouth and on the tongue. And the image comes readily of mature beech with a clearing into which sunlight pours, suggesting a cupped space, a ringed quietness, downtime.

There is such a place in the townland of Tawley, Co. Leitrim, which hosts a seventeenth-century Mass rock and baptismal font where we christened Saorlaith. It seemed the perfect place to come into a clearing in ourselves and find refreshment walking across the thick

carpet of beechnuts, then making our way
to a nearby glamping site to continue the
celebrations which Teresa recalled in a haiku:

> christening day –
> flavour of wild garlic
> on Teapot Lane

'What makes the desert beautiful', said the
little prince, 'is that somewhere it hides
a well', an oasis with trees and shade and
the sound of water in an unlikely place.
The Madonna in the trees marks out such
a still point, a centre for those who might
imagine her listening in to some stirring in
herself – a memory of leaves communing
with wind perhaps, or moisture rising.

Saorlaith must be six by now but we
remember her welcome into the universe
story with the anointed one at its centre
and the scent of wild garlic carrying us
away.

BAKING BREAD

I am old enough to remember my
mother trying to extricate her hands
from the doughy mess on a floury board
that would become our daily bread.

That was before the arrival of the sliced
pan with its official commendation by
the trinity of Johnson, Mooney and
O'Brien. The new technology meant one
less chore for my mother but it banished
the rousing smell of fresh bread from the
house.

On Saturday evenings she peeled apples
for a tart, then laid them on a bed of
pastry, added cloves, a mound of sugar
and overlaid it all with a blanket of thin
pastry; then a few stabbings to let the
steam out and a quick prayer.

Somewhere along the line, an apple tart from an industrial bakery must have been introduced and the home-made one with its ritual of last supper overtones displaced. Not that we thought of hers in such terms but in hindsight it was as close as you'd get to 'this is for you, take and eat'.

Her hands moved easily over the flour-strewn table, worked the sticky substance into a parcel of dough and marked it with a cross. When it was done she would tap the bottom for a sound that said 'done'. Reassurance. The cake of bread was then wrapped in a damp cloth and allowed to cool. It was all grace, though we would never have known to use that word. Bread it was. You could build a home around it.

RED SHOES

I take out your red shoes and look
again at your last pair, the ones I
saved from the slide to the skip. I just
thought them worth saving, so much of
you in them yet, I suppose, well worn to
the shape of your foot, deeply creased,
the pull tab of one zipper missing.

Today they resurfaced for me on meeting
an artist in the Botanic Gardens who was
laying out shoes in a half circle around
a tree. On enquiring, she told me that
it was an installation inspired by her
daughter who died forty years ago and
this range of footwear in different sizes
meant to trace her progress down the
years.

These are what she would have worn in
the course of her life – bootees, slippers,
wellies, trainers, heels, flip-flops, satin
ballet shoes, ski boots, sandals. 'She
has lived all these years,' her mother
explained. 'She's not a child. I think of
her as a forty-year-old woman and this
sculptural arrangement is, in a way, to
honour her.'

I thought of footsteps and dance steps
and a female Hermes with wings on her
heels flitting between drop-off points,
wingtips my old mother could have done
with to steady her as she wavered down
the street to the shops; all those end-of-
life repeat journeys in her red shoes.

I did return to see the shoe fest in the
grass but could only imagine a lifetime of
footsteps that never touched down.

FRUITS AND NUTS

We love the flowering stage, new leaf, petal and the clustered 'eyes' of members of the daisy family meeting ours. Of course, their showing off is not primarily for us but to draw the attention of their specific pollinator – butterfly, hoverfly, moth, beetle, honeybee. Still, we have loved flowers from first sight and can hardly imagine any special occasion without their company.

But how quickly we lose interest as their petals fade and fall away and we don't notice them anymore. Yet this is when the real work is happening for them as they produce their fruit and disperse their seeds.

Those who have paid attention to the whole ballet (and not left after the first act) have some sense of what wonders the plant is performing – how intricate the steps, how delicate the timing – while the others go for the show and miss the performance! We just haven't looked. We swoon before the shape and colour and the patterning of stigma and stamen but have no eyes for the business end of the plant's life.

I thought of that recently as I remembered evenings waiting on a bus outside St James's Hospital, when completely unbidden the word 'beauty' would arrive. Not that visiting a hospital is evidently beautiful but something in me must have recognised that in my mother's coming to the end of her dance, her inner beauty was being revealed. It is late September now, the anniversary of her fall.

ADLESTROP

You may believe time is linear and that the end comes at the end, but what happens when you draw aside for a moment and see how it feels to stop?

Sometimes the moment is made for you. The car breaks down in the month of May and you find yourself on a country road surrounded by hedges of hawthorn blossom with its delicate fragrance and a welter of bird voices. Something close to what Edward Thomas experienced when his train stopped for no apparent reason at a small station called Adlestrop, 'And for that minute a blackbird sang / Close by, and round him, mistier, / Farther and farther, all the birds / Of Oxfordshire and Gloucestershire.'

The journey broken, the mad rush forward to what comes next is halted. Now that you have stopped you might even look inside at how you are, not sniffing and moving on but letting be and allowing your inner weather to change under your gaze.

Time need not be your master. All those interruptions – slow traffic, red lights, breakdowns – can be gifts of the best kind because they give you back to yourself in a flicker of awareness. They dare you to stay right where you are with the initial feeling of annoyance until you discover a constriction in yourself loosening. You open a window and breathe, suddenly not overly concerned about what happens next as you tune into the music of what is happening now. And it feels good.

A MESSENGER

*I*n a strange way, the sign 'Collection Point' reminds me of how life comes to us in fragments, bits of conversation, destinations – arrivals and departures, unrealised good intentions like those creatures whose lives we meant to study ...

We start out walking; those first bumpy steps and falls; later we find we can run. Then we discover something called distance, the space between here and there and what lies in between, busy streets and parks and dogs; and the feeling of tired legs when still a long way from home.

When we are lost in a dream or in a folktale it's often a wise child who takes us by the hand. Today, she is the Swedish schoolgirl, Greta Thunberg, who is trying to wake the adults up, to help us remember who we are and that this is our home, because it is late now and the fire engine is screaming outside. It is screaming but we are wearing headsets and have tuned out of what is happening to the world.

So we need to start walking again – intentionally. Not simply to get fit but to reconnect with our earth, to bridge the gap between ourselves and other creatures, not allow it to get any wider, for this rupture will surely break our hearts, and irretrievably. We must walk to remind ourselves how close we are to the edge and how much 'the God who walks at evening in the garden' is missing us.

YOU CALLED

*I*n Giovanni Bellini's *Christ Giving His Blessing*, a rather fragile man raises his right hand to bless, a hand showing the infected wound where the nail has been. This is the risen Christ, the painter suggests, who cannot dispense with the marks of suffering, including the thorny bramble of mental anguish round his head. He cuts a forlorn figure with his sea-green eyes that do not hold your gaze though he will bless you if you like, send you on your way with a slight wave.

Is this not what blessing means? To reach out to, look after – what Earth does for us like the good mother she is.

In Bellini's painting, love is not strong in the usual sense but reticent, shy, almost

self-conscious. It begins by showing one's
hand, coming close yet hanging back,
no more intrusive than a coin offered
to make some transaction complete or
a coy breeze with its arm around your
shoulder.

'God bless,' Samuel Beckett is reported
to have said to some visitors by way of
goodbye which rankled with one of them
who didn't understand what the words
intended to say. In short, that something
matters.

Let it matter that you called, that we
had this conversation, raised a glass and
that it ended with a homely valediction.
And from one's weak side, too, the side
that won't heal and can't forget. Still
something for the journey, a keepsake to
start you off. A blessing – may our being
here have mattered.

COPYRIGHT ACKNOWLEDGEMENTS

Excerpts on pp. 15, 53, 85 from 'Canal Bank Walk', 'Innocence', 'To the Man After the Harrow' by Patrick Kavanagh are taken from *Collected Poems*, edited by Antoinette Quinn (Allen Lane, 2004) by kind permission of the Trustees of the Estate of the late Katherine B. Kavanagh, through the Jonathan Williams Literary Agency.

Excerpt on p. 25 from 'Blackbird' by R.S. Thomas is taken from *Uncollected Poems*, Hexham, UK: Bloodaxe Books, 2013. Used with permission.

Excerpt on pp. 38–9 from 'From Blossoms' by Li-Young Lee is taken from *Rose*. Copyright © 1986 by Li-Young Lee. Reprinted with the permission of The

Permissions Company, LLC on behalf of BOA Editions Ltd., www.boaeditions.org.

Excerpt on p. 55 from 'The Trees of My Childhood' by Edith Södergran is taken from *Complete Poems,* translated by David McDuff, Hexham, UK: Bloodaxe Books, 1984, 1992. Used with permission.

Excerpt on pp. 56–7 from 'Giuseppe' by Roderick Ford is taken from *The Shoreline of Falling*, Cork: Bradshaw Books, 2005.

Excerpt on p. 83 from 'Bush Fire – New South Wales' by Jean O'Brien is taken from *Fish on a Bicycle: New & Selected Poems*, Clare: Salmon Publishing, 2016.

Excerpt on p. 91 from 'Two Poems for Anne' by John Feehan is taken from *Background to a Poem for Hui-Tsung*, Cape Town: Salesian Press, 1974.

165 / Copyright Acknowledgements